OLD FASHIONED FOOTBALL

For Secondary Schools in the Twenty-first Century

Discipline, Organization, Simplicity, and
Fundamentals Are the Bedrock for the Successful
Implementation of Sound Football Programs

Dr. Marvin A. Martin

LIL' DAN'L

iUniverse, Inc.
Bloomington

Old Fashioned Football For Secondary Schools in the Twenty-first Century

iUniverse books may be ordered through booksellers or by contacting:

iUniverse
1663 Liberty Drive
Bloomington, IN 47403
www.iuniverse.com
1-800-Authors (1-800-288-4677)

ISBN: 978-1-4759-2705-4 (sc)
ISBN: 978-1-4759-2706-1 (e)

Printed in the United States of America

iUniverse rev. date: 05/18/2012

Contents

Foreword

"I believe you will be successful in life because of where you came from, not in spite of it."

Coach Marvin Martin said those words to me on the first day of football practice in 1957. It was my sophomore year at Daniel Webster High School. As a fullback in 1957 and 1958, and the Oklahoma–Texas Oil Bowl game, I observed Coach Martin and his staff as they resurrected the program of that small high school when they played in the toughest conference in Oklahoma.

Coach Martin not only taught the game, but he built character in each of us players by the example he set. It is a privilege to have played for him.

Even though we were a generation apart, we both grew up in the oil refinery neighborhood in West Tulsa. He was my coach, my teacher, and later my mentor when I began my career as a teacher-coach, just as he had years before. He certainly had a profound impact on my life and career.

As I begin my forty-fifth year of coaching high school football, I am constantly reminded of the basic fundamental principles and beliefs he has instilled in me, both as a player and later as a coach.

Dr. Martin taught me to respect my profession and to respect my role as a teacher in the lives of young men that I work with each day. He taught me to believe in myself and others will believe in me as well. He taught me, "If you don't have a dream, how are you going to make a dream come true?"

Marv, I am living proof of a man living his dream, and I have you to thank for it. It was a privilege to have played for you, learned from you, and participated in a small way in your book.

Your friend always,

Ronald Dale Lancaster
Head Football Coach
Broken Arrow High School
Broken Arrow, Oklahoma

Preface

I enjoyed coaching from Oklahoma to California before pursuing a doctorate in educational administration and within those experiences were many opportunities to learn from the best, particularly those from the heyday of Bud Wilkinson, Bear Bryant, Bowden Wyatt, General Neyland, and Darrell Royal. In addition, the philosophies and some fundamentals from Coach Paul Young of Muskogee, Marshall Milton, and George Broad of Tulsa Webster have been mixed with my own to form a sound football system for secondary schools. My basic thrust is to mix the philosophies of simplicity, fundamentals, and repetition of execution into an old-fashioned melting pot for championship flavor!

Acknowledgments

This book about football may appear to be fragmented. The preface and foreword may not fit into the logical scheme of things. However, I must express my appreciation to the many people who helped me to achieve success along the way, and I have tried to relate a meaningful story about the interaction I experienced with each of them as my way of saying, "Thank you."

For example, Dr. Marshall Ishmael, a lifetime friend, helped me prepare academically for my doctor's degree in education, and Dr. C.T. Prigmore helped me to land my first and only position in higher education.

But finally, to my family—Eula, Doug, and Chazz—I dedicate this book for the many times they have supported me and aided me with my endeavor, and in some cases to the detriment of their own dreams. Without the efforts of my daughter, Chazz, the transfer of this book from my house to the publisher would have been unlikely.

Thank you, all!
Marvin A. Martin
Doctor of Educational Administration

Introduction

In observing today's football coaching techniques on the high school level, I have noticed that some coaches try to follow college and even pro football coaches' sophisticated methods, such as elaborate signals and a multitude of plays. It seems to me that on the high school level, the "KISS" (Keep It Simple Stupid) technique should only be as sophisticated as the boys who are new to the game. Fancy signals, etc., which are confusing to say the least, just add unnecessary stress.

With this in mind, I am introducing a straightforward approach—based on sound plays, sound fundamentals, hard workouts, discipline, and repetition—so that each player has an automatic response under game conditions.

Part 1

The Shoulders upon Which I Stood

I n 1945, my last few months of World War II, I was a member of the construction and repair shop aboard a floating dry dock birthed in Leyte Gulf in the Philippines. We were watching a movie and during the intermission and the newsreel was about Oklahoma A&M College playing in a football bowl game. Bob Fenimore was the star for Oklahoma. At that point, I decided to go to college, play football, and become a coach! During my high school days at Webster in 1940, Glenn Dobbs was my hero. He was playing for the University of Tulsa. My best friend, Frank Bohlander, and I walked from West Tulsa to Skelly Stadium, approximately ten miles, to watch Dobbs kick, pass, and run with the ball. Our high school coach, Marshall Milton, had arranged for us to gain free admittance. Our names were on a list at the gate! Dobbs later became the University of Tulsa's coach.

My first coaching job was as Collinsville High School's line coach, where I earned $2,800 per year. I was so anxious to absorb everything I could that my wife bought me a wire recorder and Paul Young, the greatest high school coach in Oklahoma, gave me permission to record speeches at the Oklahoma High School Coaches Clinic. Coach Pappy Waldorf of Oklahoma A&M told me to turn off the recorder. Later, Coach Biggie Munn told me I could return to my recording and that Waldorf's philosophy was no secret to anyone anyway.

During my two years (1951–52) at Collinsville, we invited Coach Darrel Royal, then the backfield coach at the University of Tulsa (under the leadership of Coach Buddy Brothers) to be the speaker at our annual football banquet. Among the many things I learned from Coach Royal, who later became famous at the University of Texas, was his philosophy on field position and quarterback play-calling.

As high school principal and football coach at Collinsville High School, our superintendent of schools, Hal Wilson, allowed me to name the head football coach for the 1952 season. Coach Frank Herald of Jenks, Oklahoma, who put Jenks High School football on the map, so to speak, had an assistant coach named Rosy Davis who played football at Mississippi State under the head coach who played for General Robert Neyland. Being a very good friend, Coach Herald allowed me to "steal" Rosy Davis who installed the Tennessee single wing, the same system that was used at the University of Tennessee.

In 1952 I returned to my alma mater, Tulsa Daniel Webster High School, as assistant football coach for a four-year tenure. We ran the Tennessee single wing.

At the time, Webster was suffering from the lack of discipline and new coaches in both basketball and football. (The wrestling program was an exception due to an experienced coach, Curtis Turner.)

After several losing seasons, Dr. Harry Broad elevated me to the head football position. Special recognition goes to Dr. T.H. Broad, principal of Daniel Webster High School, and Coach Jack Howard, who was elevated to vice principal the year I became head coach. Without their cooperative attitude and staunch support, our athletic program would have remained ineffective.

With the rising fame of Coach Bud Wilkinson, during my second year as head coach at Webster we switched back to the Wilkinson split T and the wing T with the rollout and pitchout as advocated by my assistant coach, George Barnett. This was the beginning of my admiration for Oklahoma football.

It would be remiss of me not to mention other groups that had influence on our team's success. It is one of the things that boosted our morale significantly: the cheerleading squad, the pep squad, the football queen, the band, and the girlfriends of the athletes at Tulsa Webster High School. Sharon Lancaster, Sharon Saunders, Patty Watwood, Peggy Watwood, and Martine Klinefelter were some of the young ladies who played critical roles in helping us rebuild not only the football team's morale but also the entire school's morale.

Other groups and individuals that played important support roles for the athletes were Buckie Rudd, our manager and those who helped him during game time including our team physician, Dr. Elvin Davis, who volunteered his services and was at every home game. In particular I would like to note the contributions of Virgil "Onions" Martin that were so valuable that we could not have successfully turned the athletic program around if he had not organized the Webster Blue T football program! As an example, we took nine freshmen from his Blue T football program and they became varsity first-team players in 1956! We won one game and lost nine, but those players developed into leaders in all sports on or before their senior year and defeated Edison High School the final game of the year at Tulsa's Skelly stadium. Edison Eagles had had an undefeated season up to that game and a great coaching staff! Coaches included Ralph Parker, F.A. Dry, Bill Grove, H.J. Green, and Tom Langhiem. Jim Sellers was athletic director. Onions was not only the Blue T head coach but also my brother. He was assisted by James "Cootie" Arnold.

Members of the Webster High School football team during the rebuilding years were Jerry Admire, Larry Bohannon, Leroy Chandler, John Estes, Bill Gibson, Gene Hart, Jim Hart, Dan Howard, Ron Lancaster, Larry Lawrence, Doug Martin, Tom Maxwell, Bucky Rudd, Duane Sams, Glenn Sams, Don Scroggins, Bryce Smith, Gary Smith, Dave Sparks, and Sammy Terry.

The coachers were Jack Howard, George Burnett, Gene Ross, Bill Cale, Wally Knapp, Harold Biesel, and Bill Allen. Gene Ross and Bill Cale were not only excellent coaches but also splendid educators.

The major portion of this football system is copied from great coaches during the heyday of Bud Wilkinson, Bear Bryant, Bowden Wyatt, and General Neyland. However, the philosophies and some fundamentals from

Coach Paul Young of Muskogee and Marshal Milton of Tulsa Webster High School have been mixed with all of the above to form a sound football system for secondary schools of Oklahoma and Texas.

Since the writer worked with coach Ron Lancaster for two years while at Jenks, much of Ron's philosophy is mixed into the old-fashioned melting pot for championship flavor.

The basic thrust is to continue with the philosophies of Coach Wilkinson's simplicity and Coach Neyland's fundamentals and repetition of execution.

Coaches Gomer Jones and Bud Wilkinson allowed me to observe spring football practice in May 1956. Coach Bill Allen took my last class of the day while my freshman son Doug and I observed the OU practice at 2:30 PM each day. Doug was quite impressed to meet Tommy McDonald, Eddie Crowder, and other members of the OU family.

Coach Wilkinson organized his classroom so that each coach was assigned a ten-yard zone around the football field.

Coaching Zones

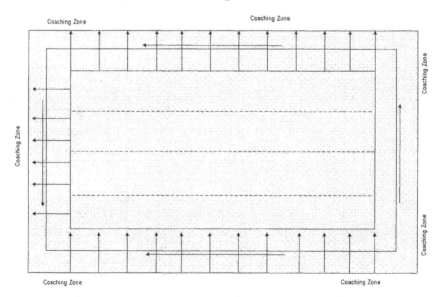

It is noteworthy to mention that all fundamentals were limited to a certain time frame and all hands were busily engaged in each drill. There were no idle coaches or players.

I enjoyed a closer relationship with Coach Jones because of Clyde McGinnis, a graduate of OU and owner of a sporting goods store in Tulsa. I had designed a shoulder pad tree that would hold one hundred high school sized shoulder pads. Gomer allowed me to exhibit it in the university gym lobby so that other coaches could view and purchase. However, Woody West, the athletic director of Hale High School, was the only coach to purchase one. The other coaches made drawings, took pictures, and made their own trees.

Because the Webster coaching staff turned the football program around from losing to winning, and because we beat Edison High School for the second year in succession by a score of 34–14 (an undefeated team as of the date we played them), coaches Herman Ragsdale and Joe Robinson (officers in the Oklahoma High School Coaches Association) selected me to coach the Texas Oil Bowl game with Jerry Potter and Thurman Garrett as my assistants. Eddie Crowder an assistant at OU and Tommy Hudspeth, an assistant at TU were the two college recruiters who helped us select the Oklahoma players who would oppose the Texas All Stars, who were coached by two college coaches, Claud Gilstrap and Thurman Jones. (Special recognition is awarded to Dr. Joe Lemley and his 1958 Webster drafting class for their efforts in preparing the original football manual prior to the 1959 Oil Bowl Game in Wichita Falls, Texas.)

Paul Davis, my college roommate and teammate at NSU, called my attention to the huddle play, which he called the "bloody bucket." (Paul is now the proud father of the coach of the Cleveland Browns.) The first time I used the play was in 1957 against Booker T. Washington High School, coached by Art Williams. Webster defeated Washington 47–7. Early in the Oil Bowl game we used the play and scored on the Texas All Stars. Coach Crowder stated that the play made all the difference in a close game (21–14) and a run away by Texas. Coach Wilkinson also scored on the huddle play a few weeks after we had used it. Later in my career, I won the conference championship with the "bloody bucket" when our Walnut Creek, California, team defeated Piedmont, California, in the fall of 1959.

Bloody Bucket—The Huddle Play

The huddle play works best from the kickoff.

1. We return the ball to our right hash mark.
2. We use an open-face huddle.
3. I have informed the referee prior to kickoff and have given him a paper clip-marked rule book.
4. Our huddle must be formed on our side of scrimmage line.
5. Our quarterback calls "bloody bucket" when the center is ready.
6. The QB takes the center's place and looks at the opposing defense that will be near the ball!
7. The center (QB) laterals the ball to a fast back and runs downfield for a pass.
8. The ball carrier runs to the left and his teammates form the Oklahoma Alley for punt and kick-off returns.
9. A and B pick up "leakers." See diagram below.

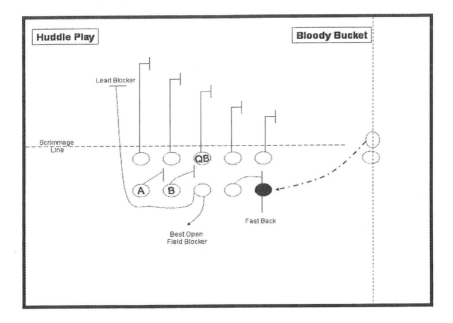

The backbone and modern concepts of Coach Ron Lancaster should be most helpful to young coaches in this century. Lancaster's championship record of achievements from Rancho Cordova, California, (sixty won and four lost in the 1960s and 1970s) to Enid, Oklahoma, in the 1970s and 1980s, and Jenks, Oklahoma, in the 1990s will serve as a testament to his achievements and championship coaching abilities. The final portion to Ron Lancaster's career is being written as you read this book since Ron will be completing his career at Muskogee High School—the home of Paul Young, the Burris boys, and Eddie Crowder.

Ron Lancaster, Bob Lancaster, and Dennit Morris, products of Tulsa Webster High School, were not only great athletes but much more: They were good human beings who accomplished more in life than being *all-star athletes!* These three gentlemen are living examples of the truth that Coach George Broad and Dr. Harry Broad taught us to believe in during the Great Depression. That is, *football is a scrimmage for later life.*

Frederick Winslow Taylor is known as the "father of scientific management," and Charles "Bud" Burnam Wilkinson utilized the philosophies of Taylor and John Dewey to manage a football practice session. Henry Ford would have been proud to see how the automobile assembly line had evolved into an athletic assembly line in 1956. Coach Wilkinson's stated goal was to organize a football practice that would emulate game conditions and then teach each and every player to "react" to the various stimuli.

The following is a brief description of a football field organized as a classroom.

Since the major objective of football is to advance the ball ten yards or more until a touchdown is scored, the field is divided into twenty five-yard strips that are fifty-three and one-third yards wide. Thus, a logical classroom would seem to be five-yard grids as shown. (See diagram on page nine.)

To be champions, the coaching staff should do the following:

1. Understand that fatigue is major concern for all coaches and players.

2. Consider the affective domain when preparing practice. The emotions of Notre Dame players caused the great Knute Rockne to achieve maximum results. However, *"One will never play better than he is able to play."*

But after the team is fundamentally sound, the coach can move players to the next level of cognitive and psychomotor by dealing with the affective domain. The ingredient is called "desire" knows what it is, but all coaches worth their salt know you can't win without desire.

A player will play as he practices! Therefore, each day one member of the staff needs to appeal to the leaders to improve over the day before. If one will do his best each day to improve over the previous practice, he will one day be a champion. A different coach should make the appeal each day for maximum effort. Also B.F. Skinner taught us that a reward after practice, such as Cokes for leaders, is a good reinforcement, or providing a cup of ice now and then, but not every day may result in reinforcing player's maximum effort at practice. Remember Skinner's pigeons! The reward must exist only now and then. Seek advice from your team physician for more data regarding rest periods and liquids.

The cognitive area is the "biggie," but we must not forget how to teach thinking animals. We must tell them what we are going to teach them. Then we must demonstrate what is to be taught. Then teach the fundamental by repetition. Then tell them what we taught. They must practice until reaction occurs. Now to organize a practice with the above philosophy within our plan, one must try to be a gestalt!

Even in retirement the men of my past have come full circle to become a part once again of my present. Every Wednesday morning, hall-of-fame coach J.V. Haney and Spirit Bank, located at 4815 S. Harvard, host a coffee and roll gabfest consisting of retired hall-of-fame coaches. After Coach Dobbs' retirement from the University of Tulsa, he joined our group. Some of the other regular members are Joe Grant, Cecil Hankins, H.J. Green, Tommy Hudspeth, Tom Langheim, John Payne, Joe Shoulders, Gene Shell, Red Rogers, Bill Grove, Jack Kiper, Dave Kragthorpe, John Phillips,

George Utley, Jim Sellers, Don Payne, Joe Lemley, Dave Kragthorpe, Jerry Billings, and Bill Allen.

One of my most unforgettable years was in 2001 when Glenn Dobbs invited me to join his golf group at South Lakes near Jenks, Oklahoma. Gene Shell, John Paul, Coach Dobbs, and sometimes Red Rogers played with us on Tuesdays and Thursdays. I have in my trophy case a letter with $6.00 I won at our last meeting before Coach Dobbs developed health problems and was no longer able to play.

It is through these incredible people and events that I am led to write this book and recreate the coaching manual that defined my career.

Part 2

Organization of High School Football Practice in the Twenty-First Century

Socrates wisely suggested we define our terms if we expect to communicate. Therefore, a well-organized, efficient coach will organize each practice to resemble game conditions and teach each player to react to those specific conditions. *React* is the operative word and from Bloom's Taxonomy we must borrow the three domains:

    A. Cognitive;
    B. Affective;
    C. Psychomotor.

The football player has not the time for thinking or cognition; he must function at level C, the psychomotor or reactive level (i.e., when feeling physical pressure from the left, he moves toward the pressure).

Definitions of the terms *effective* and *efficient* need to be understood by the players. *Effective* is doing the right thing. *Efficient* is doing the right thing right.

A sound football coach will win more than he loses by following the above plans.

Punting and Covering Drill

All players report to the practice field thirty minutes prior to practice time and jog one-half mile prior to exercises. Those who skip the honor-system jog will pay double penalty after practice when identified. Enter into pre-practice punting and covering drill until coach blows whistle two times.

Punt and Cover Drill # 1

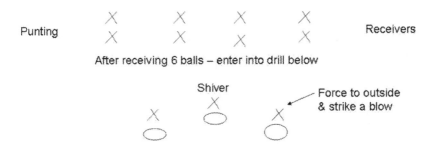

After receiving six balls –
Enter into drill on following page.

Punt and Cover Drill #2

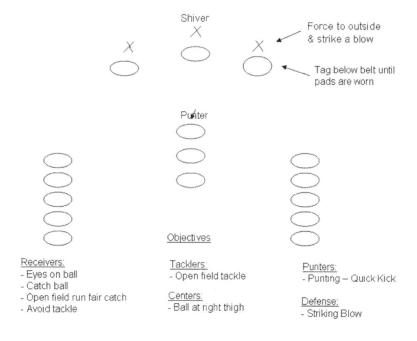

Football Practice by Dividing the Staff into Two Units

Since fatigue and morale are related and critical factors in football practice and games, the following plans are proposed to obtain the maximum efficiency during the opening sessions of August football practice for a high school of 3A, 4A, 5A, and 6A classification.

The staff should be divided by defensive/offensive groups or groups of first and third vs. second and fourth, plus all others being assigned to practice with the third on odd days and fourth on even days.

Coaches are divided by school colors. In this case, red team coaching will be the responsibility for first- and third-team players and white team coaching will be the responsibility of second-, fourth- and all others. However, absent players from the first and third will be replaced from third and fourth team members unless an exception is made by the assistant head coach who has the responsibility for keeping the rank board updated prior to 6:00 PM each day.

Following is an insert as an example of a one-week football practice used in the 1990s by Coach Lancaster at Jenks, Oklahoma.

Monday

3:10–3:20   Warm-ups

3:20–3:30   Special Period
                       Punters—kick-offs—conversion
                       Receivers—receivers—conversion

3:30–3:50   Groups

Ends
1. Slow play option (sweat)
2. Deliver blow on end
3. Squeeze off tackle
4. Pinch technique

Linebackers
1. Stance and Hit
2. Scrape technique
3. Offside gap
4. Read steps and drop (screens/draws)

Tackles
1. Deliver blow (read)
2. Pinch technique
3. Slant to/away
4. Containment of quarterback

Nose
1. Deliver blow and read
2. Pursuit
3. Quick read and reaction
4. Slant technique

Offensive Backs

1. Quarterbacks (steps, read, pitch)
2. Halfbacks (ball handling, blocks)
3. Fullbacks (block Linebackers bone path)

Offensive Line

1. Direction cut off
2. Co-op
3. Finish block

Defensive Backs

1. Recognition
2. Contain response

3:50–4:10	Team offense
4:10–4:30	Team defense
4:30–6:30	Films (for coaches only)

Wednesday

3:10–3:25	Warm-ups
3:25–3:30	Kick-off team and conversion
3:30–3:50	Group
3:50–4:05	Seven on seven skeleton pass defense; pits offense and defense
4:10–4:40	Team defense

(ten min.) Shade and base
(ten min.) 53/54 and 59 pinch
(ten min.) Live scrimmage
1. Deliver blow → ultimate each play

2. Explode to ball
3. Execute properly
4. Total concentration

4:40–5:10   Team offense (two)
                 (15 min.) two team offense polish
1. Sprint to and from huddle, recognize defense, etc.
2. Complete explosion off ball
3. Execute offside blocking
                 (15min.) Team offense scrimmage
1. Sub by position
2. Complete concentration during drills

4:30   Films

Part 3

Martin Coaching Manual

Contents Coaching Manual

Schedule Sample

Varsity

September 12	Friday	McGuinness	Home	8:00 PM
September 19	Friday	McLain	Away	8:00 PM
September 26	Friday	Kelley	Home	8:00 PM
October 3	Friday	McLain	Away	8:00 PM
October 10	Friday	Muskogee	Home	8:00 PM

Schedule Sample

Junior Varsity

September 12	Friday	McGuinness	Home	5:00 PM
September 19	Friday	McLain	Away	5:00 PM
September 26	Friday	Kelley	Home	5:00 PM
October 3	Friday	McLain	Away	5:00 PM
October 10	Friday	Muskogee	Home	5:00 PM

Coaching Assignments Sample

Coach A	Offensive coordinator
Coach B	Defensive coordinator
Coach C	Quarterbacks
Coach D	Special teams

Chapter 1

Open Letter to the Football Players

We are striving to produce perfect teams which stand for winning games, high moral character, sound educational values in life, and the pleasure and enjoyment of participation and competition.

The athletes who have achieved championship performance have done so through a terrific amount of sacrifice and self-discipline. They are willing to "pay the price" for playing on a good ball club; they have worked hard and lived in accordance with training rules to achieve maximum efficiency in their performance. The degree of greatness which you may achieve depends on your willingness "to put out" and faithfully follow the rules of championship living.

No young man can smoke, drink, or chase women and be as fine an athlete as he would be without these handicaps.

Dates

At the proper time and place, dating is part of social growth and development. The attraction of one sex for the other has been present since the creation of man and will be here when we are gone. When a young man's social life and dating become his primary objectives, he can no longer give his undivided attention to the game. In some cases, the right girl may be a good influence on an athlete if she has his best interests at heart. It will be to your advantage not to have dates during the season on any night preceding a class day or a game. Do not in any way violate training rules on your dates.

Hours
Be home by 10:00 any night before school day and midnight on others.

Eligibility to Play and Earn a Letter

Grades
Each boy must maintain a passing grade in at least three solid subjects. Examples include history, English, math, science, chemistry, etc. Not solid subjects include phys. ed., stagecraft, music, etc.

Attendance
A boy must be in attendance at least 80 percent of the total school time (four times a week). On the day you are absent, you will not be allowed to practice.

Age
Any boy who has reached his nineteenth birthday before September 1 of each football year will be ineligible for high school competition.

Earning a letter
A boy must complete the season in good standing and play in at least eighteen quarters in order to earn a letter.

Policies and Slogans

1. Horseplay will not be tolerated at any time.
2. Stealing of equipment will not be tolerated.
3. No cursing is allowed on or off the field.
4. Show respect for your teammates' rights.

5. Remain on your feet at all times on the field.
6. When not participating, listen and watch.
7. Be on the field ready to go to work on time. If an hour early, work on weaknesses.
8. Don't be an "alibi" Ike.
9. Do what you are told to the best of your ability.
10. Doesn't miss practice without permission. Cutting practice will not be tolerated.
11. You must be a gentleman in both buildings. If you are a troublemaker, you will be eliminated.
12. No one has a position on the team until he proves himself to be the best man for the job.
13. Everyone will be expected to work hard, *top boys more so.*
14. A poor attitude on the part of any player is inexcusable.
15. If you have a complaint, bring it to the football coach.
16. Each player must have a medical examination signed by his parents.
17. No spectators will be allowed in the dressing rooms during games.
18. We will have no time to visit with friends or relatives during practice sessions.
19. Be on the field and busy by 2:35 PM during regular practice sessions.
20. Any player who is sidelined by the doctor should report to the practice area and observe unless otherwise instructed.
21. Helmets will be worn at all times. Never throw or sit on them.
22. Benzoin and powder your feet daily.
23. Football is a man's game. You will be treated as a man and will be expected to act like a man.

Axioms

1. A squad that does not stick together falls apart under pressure.
2. Bravery escapes more dangers than cowardice.
3. You will play like you practice.
4. Bounce off the ground. It discourages your opponents.

5. Be ready for a short (onside) kick.
6. Block all opponents away from balls that are punted to your team until you hear the whistle.
7. Every time you make them fumble and we recover, we gain at least fifty yards.
8. Never pass up a wrong-colored jersey.

Practice Sessions

Football practice will begin *(your date)*. Physical examinations will be given August 20 at 2:00 PM. Equipment will be checked out August 23 from 9:30 AM to 4:30 PM. A squad meeting will be held August 24 at 10:00 AM.

Practice will start officially August 25 and last from 7:30 AM to 9:30 AM. Afternoon workout is from 3:30 to 5:30. We will follow this practice schedule Monday through Saturday until school starts. Then we will practice from 2:35–5:15 PM

Upon entering the football practice area, each boy will run *two* laps and work on fundamentals until the first whistle has blown. Then he follows the plan of the day, which will be posted daily.

Travel

All equipment will be cleaned, neatly packed, and ready to go during the sixth hour on the day of the game. The varsity will be allowed to go home after the bags are packed. Anyone seen in the building or downtown will forfeit the varsity privileges.

The coaches, managers, and players will wear clothes within keeping of a well-groomed man. Slacks, sports shirts, and jackets are suggested for players and managers.

All personnel will ride to and from our destination on the school bus.

There will be no loud noises or horseplay of any kind on the bus. Think about the game. Remember that you are representatives from

Daniel Webster High School, whether you are eating in a restaurant or riding in a bus.

Upon return, do the following:

1. Carry your *own* bag into the gym.
2. Unpack and hang gear on your hook.

Grading System

+ 2—Carried out his assignment well; great second effort.

+ 1—Carried out his assignment well; no second effort.

  0—Carried out his assignment. No criticism.

- 1—Carried out his assignment; poor block.

- 2—Missed the assignment.

Goals and Purpose of Football

Our purpose for having competitive football is to make better athletes and better young men out of boys. We believe that if something is worth doing at all, it is worth doing well, and therefore we will demand that the participants do their best at all times. If a man does his very best, no one can criticize. To play well, one must play *hard*; and we will not accept mediocrity.

A boy representing this high school and this coaching staff will be a well-disciplined individual. We expect him to do exactly as we tell him, *precisely* when we tell him, and as *quickly* as possible, whether he agrees with us or not. Our overall policy is to treat each individual firmly, but fairly. I feel that we are paid to coach boys and not to court them.

Every boy will have a fair opportunity to make the team if he lives up to his responsibilities.

To play football for Daniel Webster High School is a privilege, and only those who deserve it will be allowed that privilege.

We are convinced that a school cannot separate the athletic program from the academic building and the attitudes of the student body. Therefore, we insist that every football player be a living example of a good life no matter where you may find him. We want him to be vicious, a well-conditioned and a well-trained individual on the field of play, but in the classroom we want him to play the role of a gentleman. Fritz Chrisler once said, "You can be as tough as nails and still be a gentleman."

We can and will win if we are willing to subordinate our desires to those of the group and take coaching readily and willingly.

Physical Condition

Physical condition is the most neglected and underrated phase of a football program. An all-American is mediocre without superb physical condition. We will get into top condition by doing the following:

1. Sprints.
2. Punting and covering drills.
3. Hustling every minute we are on the field.
4. Getting enough sleep. A boy should have at least nine hours a day. To bed at 10:00 PM, awake at 7:00 AM. Sleep in your own bed and alone if possible.
5. Food tube must be eliminating properly.
6. Eating three wholesome meals each day. Do not skip breakfast.
7. Relaxing one hour after practice before eating.
8. Avoid the following foods in excess: grease, pastries, sweets, and cakes. Do not overeat!

Injuries

An athlete who is in top condition seldom gets hurt. Learn to absorb punishment. Don't be a "cry baby or a Band-Aid idiot."

Injuries are caused by the following: poor condition, improper technique, mediocre desire, accidents; and poor equipment.

All injuries should be reported to the coach responsible for the first-aid room. If necessary, he will refer your case to a doctor. If you go to our doctor, we will pay the bill. Where you choose your own doctor, you are responsible.

If you are injured to the point of taping, you can't practice. If *no practice,* then *you can't play* on Friday night.

Care of Injuries

Cuts and hand scratches — Cleanse well and apply antiseptic.

Bruises to bone and muscles — Apply cold pack immediately to stop swelling, also an ankle wrap may be necessary. After twelve to twenty-four hours, apply hot, moist heat. The heat lamp is second best. Care for your injuries at home and not during practice time. If you skip practice to care for an injury, then you will not be well in time for the game.

Blisters – Prevention is the secret; use tough skin daily. The trainer will burst blisters, if necessary, and will cut away dead tissue. Then, he will apply antiseptic and bandage.

The man who plays hard and hits instead of being hit is less likely to receive an injury. A boy who really wants to play will not be kept out by minor bruises, scratches, and strains. *"Hitch up your guts and be a man."*

Important Football Rules

The kicking game The receiving team may not advance the ball on extra points. Always cover the ball, and don't advance it from behind the goal line unless you can reach the twenty-yard line. Signal for a fair catch if the ball is high and the defense is near. (Hand straight up.) The receiving team must have an opportunity to catch a punt or kicked ball.

The punting game A blocked punt may be advanced by anyone. Don't touch the kicker. The kicking team can recover it but not advance it. The kicking team should not kill the ball unnecessarily.

Lateraling Anyone may receive and advance a lateral if caught in mid air. Only the offense can advance grounded laterals.

Fumbles Cover all fumbles and if caught in the air *score*. Steal the ball. Force fumbles—tackle through the ball.

Men in motion Must move away from or parallel to the line of scrimmage. Flankers must be on or at least one yard off the line of scrimmage. *The offense must be set one full second before the ball is snapped.* The exception is a man (one only) in motion.

Passing Offensive guards, tackles, and centers never go down field until the ball is thrown. Never block or interfere with a secondary man after the ball is thrown—unless it is caught.

Defending against passes

1. Rush the passer with all your might and block him down after the ball is thrown.
2. The defense is allowed to push, pull, lift, grasp, knock down, or ward off any offensive man between him and the ball.

3. Do not interfere with receivers down field on passes unless you are fighting for the ball.

4. Only one forward pass is allowed.

5. The passer must be on or behind the line of scrimmage.

Substitutions May be made during following: timeout, clock stopped, incomplete pass, change of period, injured man, penalty, referee discretion, out of bounds, and after touchdowns.

1. Substitutes will be penalized for entering game after the official walks away from ball.

2. Offensive team has twenty-five seconds to move the ball.

3. A sixth time out each half may be had *only* for an injured player.

4. The holders for extra points may run, pass, or kick the ball even if a knee is down.

5. On an extra point, the ball may be placed anywhere inbounds on the three-yard line.

6. After a touchback or safety, the defending team snaps or free kicks the ball respectively.

Clipping You must make initial contact with your head, shoulder, or hip in front of the opponent or receive a fifteen-yard clipping penalty.

Offensive holding Keep your hands in contact with your numerals and avoid holding penalties.

Chapter 2

Theory of Martin Offense

The purpose of offensive football is to advance the ball an average of four yards per down. We are convinced that the T-formation is the simplest and best method of achieving this purpose.

Description: Holes are numbered on outside hips of linemen.

Offensive Formation and Hole Numbers

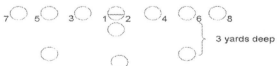

Offensive Formation

Balanced T with Flankers
Line Splits vary from 6" to 3'
Backs distance from the line will vary with their quickness and speed

Fundamentals

Shoulder Blocking—Explode forward with a "bull neck."

1. Drive the head at the opponent's belt and slide it to one side before contact. Keep the head and eyes up.
2. Aim where you expect your opponent to be – not where he was.
3. Take a short preliminary step if the opponent is on the line.
4. When contact is made with the right shoulder, the right leg should furnish the drive and the foot must be directed toward the center of the body.
5. Drive through the man with feet spread using quick piston-like steps to maintain contact.
6. Turn your opponent *only* after you receive pressure. Keep your hands in contact with your jersey and elbows spread like wings.
7. When two opponents are in the same zone, expect a cross charge. Take a "six" step with your inside foot and aim at the first opponent's pelvis. Be ready to block the second man when they cross.

Double Team Blocking—Power and post.

1. **Post man**—Stop the charge of the defensive man by driving your head into the stomach of the opponent and change to your inside shoulder as you feel the pressure from your power man.
2. **Power man**—Take a preliminary step forward with your outside foot and use a pivot twist step toward your post man, driving the man laterally.
3. The blocker's inside arms should overlap and keep his hips in contact.

Body Blocking—

1. When within one yard of the defensive man, spring from one foot and aim your hip at the opponent's numeral.
2. Throw your arm and shoulder across the front of the opponent.

3. Speed is all important. Follow through with a grabbing movement pinning the opponent's legs between the V of your upper and lower body.

Tackling—Be in a quarter-eagle stance and under control within striking distance of the ball carrier.

1. Act like a blocker except drive your head through the ball and clasp your hands around the opponent's legs—lift and drive. *Never allow the man to fall forward.*
2. Tackle through the ball carrier. Not to him, but *through* him.

Passing—By the quarterback (drop back).

1. Grip the ball lightly with fingers spread on rear half, last three fingers on laces and index fingers toward end of ball.
2. Carry the ball back quickly with both hands to point behind right ear, shifting weight to rear foot.
3. Keeping nose of ball slightly up, step forward in direction of receiver.
4. Bring left hand to side for balance and protection.
5. Whip the ball with a free, overhand motion, letting weight flow from rear to front foot.
6. Try to deliver ball at head level, making receiver reach for it. If receiver is facing you, aim at his chest.
7. Let throwing arm follow through naturally.
8. Practice against rushing opponents. It's throwing *under pressure* that counts. Nearly anybody can throw a ball accurately with nobody rushing him.

Passing—By the halfbacks (running pass).
Apply the same fundamentals as for the drop-back pass except for the following:

1. Delivery is made mostly with the hands and arms.
2. Make the play look like a run. Keep the ball in both hands. And *pass only when you can't run.*
3. The best play is when you throw while running toward the line of scrimmage.
4. Very little lead is necessary. Be familiar with the habits of your receivers.

Punting—The punter should get the ball off in *about two seconds* after the centering which will *consume one second*. The ball should be *kept in the air about four seconds* to allow the linemen time for coverage.

1. Assume a relaxed semi-erect position with feet several inches apart, right foot a bit forward with weight over it.
2. Extend arms as target (for center) with fingers spread and relaxed.
3. Upon receiving ball, quickly finger it into position. Place right hand toward rear and left hand toward front on opposite side.
4. Holding ball about waist level, take a short step with right foot and a normal step with left.
5. As left foot comes forward, remove balance (left) hand, and then gently remove right hand.
6. Whip kicking foot into ball, keeping knee bent until ball approaches knee level. Then snap leg out straight with toe pointed down.
7. Idea is to meet the ball on instep (but not toe) at about knee height.
8. Keep eyes on ball from start to finish and end up on toe. Avoid jumping into air.

Centering for the punt—

1. Take a good stance that is comfortable.
2. Place the right hand under the front of the ball with the thumb on top and place the left hand on the opposite side. The left hand guides. The right hand does the work.

3. Whip the ball back with good wrist action. Hand must follow through. Bring the arms and head up quickly and prepare to move to block. At practice start at five yards and work up to thirteen. We will kick from ten yards.

Signal System and Automatics

The quarterback will call the desired play and call left half set left or right if a flanker is desired. The center will line up on the ball and then all others leave the huddle with a handclap, yell, "Hey!" and sprint to their desired positions ready to run the play on set or hut. The line and backs will be in a three-point stance and ready to go.

Example: #1-24 Left half set left on *hut*. (Break—set—hut)

Example: #1-24 Left half set right on *set*. (Break—set)

All hands move off together.

Checking Signals When Not Huddling

1. The quarterback will softly call out the new play.
2. A false call will be given occasionally, but the quarterback will notify the team while huddling.
3. The jump pass signal will be any number preceded by a one.

By anyone
Ice—Pass Interception
Ki Yi—Lateral to me
By defensive captain
Ho Ho—Hold the ends

Red Dog—Seven man rush
By Coach Martin
Fisted hands—Quick kick
Palm over head—Punt
Both hands in pocket—Your decision

Basic Stances for Each Position

Center

1. The center sets up with his feet about parallel and grasps the ball with both hands, the laces toward the sideline.
2. The rest of his stance is the same as that of the other linemen.
3. Keep the ball out in front with body weight forward.

Linemen

1. The feet are as wide as the shoulders on a toe and instep (or heel) alignment. The legs are flexed at the knee and ready to explode.
2. The right hand is dropped off at the shoulder and moved out five inches from that point on a line inside the right foot. Both hands may be down.
3. The left forearm and wrist rest loosely inside of and below the left knee.
4. The head and eyes are up, looking down field.
5. The hips are as high as the shoulders. The shoulders are square and to the line of scrimmage.

Halfbacks—Assume a sprinter's stance

1. Feet are ten feet apart on a heel and toe alignment.
2. The down hand is placed on the ground on a line inside the rear foot with 60 percent of the body weight forward. Both hands may be down.
3. The shoulders are square to the line of scrimmage with the head and eyes up. *The tail is higher than the head.*
4. The halfbacks must be ready to explode forward and act like a ball carrier each time.

Fullback—Assume a line stance with no weight on the down hand.

1. Feet are not staggered. The arm is dropped off at the shoulder.
2. Heels are on the ground but weight is over the balls of the feet.

Quarterback—Crowd the center with the head up and shoulders square.

1. Bend the knees to get the back of the hand in the centers crotch with pressure, the other hand pointing to the ground.
2. Feet parallel and ten feet wide.

Defensive stances and charge—men who play on the line will take a stance similar to our offensive stance plus the following:

Tackles

1. Line up in a three- or four-point stance with your striking foot back and directed at the crotch of the opponent.
2. Step off with your striking foot and deliver a forearm lift with the corresponding arm. Grasp the opponent with the opposite arm.
3. Your legs need to be off the line from your offensive opponent.

Middle Guard

1. Take a stance like our offensive fullback.
2. Use the arm shiver directed at the opponent's collarbone.

Ends

1. Take a quarter-eagle stance and follow the tackle's instructions.

All other defensive personnel will take a quarter-eagle stance and move to the ball under control.

Backfield Maneuvers and Ball Exchange

The quarterback is responsible for the transfer of the ball to all backs.

Quarterback

1. Allow the hands to follow the center as you step up and out toward the scrimmage line.
2. Keep the ball belt high and on the line of scrimmage.
3. On the handoffs, lay the ball on the far pelvis of the ball carrier. (Look at the pocket.) On 23 and 24, hurry to the HB then complete your normal route.
4. On 25 and 26, hurry to the fifth or sixth hole, fake a pitchout to the wide HB and hand the ball forward to the fullback and then turn the corner and block.
5. On the pitchout, hurry to the hand-off area, slow down making the defensive end play you, and then pitch the ball head high and in front of the receiving back.
6. On the running pass, pitch the ball after the halfback has dived and then block out on the defensive #4 man.

Fullback

1. Run a route toward the offensive end except on the following:
   a. Option play—Run a route toward the outside leg of the #4 defensive man (second man standing).
   b. Fullback counter—Take a counter step and run over the ball and find daylight.
2. Keep your eyes on the point of attack; watch the *defensive* man who may tackle you.
3. Keep your inside arm high and your outside hand on your pelvis.
4. Adjust yourself to the QB on the counter and reverses. He will adjust to you on the slants.

Halfback

1. Run a route over tackle faking over the ball.
2. Keep your eyes on *the defensive man who may tackle you.*
3. Keep your inside arm high and your outside hand on your pelvis.
4. After receiving the ball, find daylight.
5. Block any defensive man who penetrates, if the ball is not meant for you.
6. When the opposite HB dives, run a route four yards deeper than the QB and turn the corner as quickly as possible.
7. On 27 and 28 stay on the outside hip of the fullback until he makes his block.
8. On the running pass, your route is between the QB and fullback and toward the line of scrimmage. Always run when you can make four yards.

Line Splits, Hole Numbers, and Blocking Rules

Symbols

Zero man — The man heading our offensive center on or off the scrimmage line.

#1 man — Next man on the line outside the zero man.

#2 man — Next man on the line outside the #1 man.

#3 man — Next man outside the #2 man.

#4 man — Next man outside the #3 man.

A defensive man will be counted if he is not deeper than one yard off the line of scrimmage or if he is in a crashing position. The responsibilities for the 0, 1, 2, 3, and 4 men are as follows: 0—center; 1s—guards; 2s—tackles; 3s—ends; 4s—backs.

RULE BLOCKING AND SLOT DEFENSE

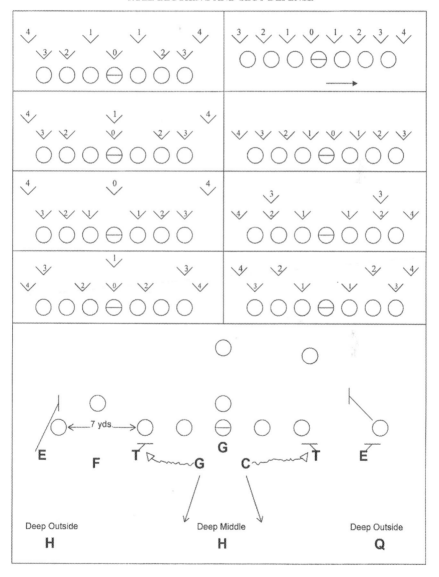

Punt Formation

1. All blockers protect to the inside and leave on the "thud" of the ball.
2. Ends stay and block on an overloaded defense.
3. Do not kill the ball unless it is bouncing toward our goal.
4. Never kill the ball inside their ten-yard line.
5. Run with a blocked punt.

Kick-off Formation

1. Never follow the same-colored jersey downfield.
2. Turn the ball carrier to the inside.
3. Always cover a kick-off.
4. Never advance a kick-off unless you can gain the twenty–yard line.
5. Expect an onside kick.

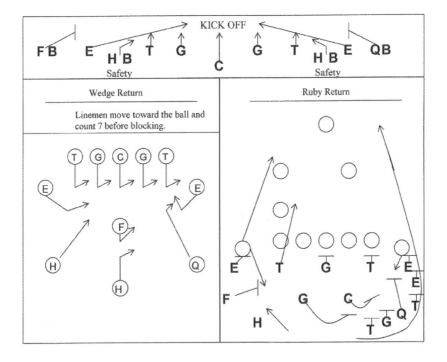

Chapter 3

Quarterback's Manual

The quarterback must do the following:

1. Understand and recognize defenses.
2. Relate our offense to each defense.
   a. Avoid the *bad play* (go quickly).
   b. Run inside, outside, reverse, or pass.
   c. Run a balanced offense. Examples:
      Inside handoff – seven times (sneak three times)
      Outside handoff – seven times
      Reverse – three times
      Pass – three times
3. Understand tactics.
   a. Score – time remaining.
   b. How many downs and how many yards?
   c. Think what the defense will do then do the opposite unless you can do the logical well:
      1) If we have one down to make eight yards, they will expect a pass. We will hit the handoff. (They will be loose.)
      2) Two downs to make two yards, they will expect a TD play. We will pick up first down with sneak or hand off.

3) Sometimes on third and short in the four-down zone we will run outside because they will expect an inside play.

4) Avoid the bad play and when we must make yards we will run one and two Q, 23, 24 sneak, or keep.

4. Be familiar with opponents.

   a. Take advantage of defensive tactics.

     1) Run around crashing ends.

     2) Run inside deep-penetrating tackles.

     3) Run around a tight line; run through a loose line.

     4) Use reverse against a sliding or angle-charging line.

     5) Use cross blocking when possible, against a hard, straight-charging line.

   b. Know who stopped your play.

     1) Use your own eyes.

     2) Get information from teammates.

   c. Run a play at an injured opponent or a substitute; throw a pass into the territory of an opponent who has just fumbled.

5. Don't waste your timeouts; use your opponent's.

6. know your position on field.

   a. From your own goal to the twenty-yard line is the *danger zone*. From the opponent's twenty-yard line to their goal is the scoring zone. The remaining area is the neutral zone.

   b. When in your danger zone, do the following:

     1) Get the ball out quickly and as safely as possible.

     2) Inside your own ten-yard line use quarterback sneak or keep and quickies with the fullback deep. Punt on third down.

     3) Inside your own five-yard line punt on second down if you have not made five yards.

   c. When in the scoring zone do the following:

     1) Use your most trusted play and the best ball carrier.

     2) When inside the opponent's ten-yard line our line must close the splits.

3) You must never fail to score inside their ten.

4) On third down and long yardage think about moving the ball to mid field for a fourth-down field goal.

QUARTERBACKS MANUAL

Q.B. MUST:

1. KNOW THE DEFENSE, DOWN, DISTANCE, TIME, SCORE AND BEST PLAY RIGHT NOW.

2. KEEP HIS ATTACK BALANCED -- DON'T BE RIGHT OR LEFT HANDED

3. RUN AT STAND UP MEN, RUN OUTSIDE IF THEY HAVE LESS THAN TWO MEN OUTSIDE OUR ENDS.

4. THINK IN TERMS OF -- THE NUMBER OF DOWNS ALLOWED TO MAKE THE NEEDED YARDAGE.

THE CHART BELOW IS THE GUIDE.

2 DOWNS	⟶ ⟵	3 DOWNS	⟶ ⟵ ⟶	4 DOWNS TO MAKE 10 YDS.	
RUN ON 3RD	RUN ON 3RD	LIMITED PASSING.	OPTIONAL	SAFE PLAYS.	BEST PLAY
AND 2 OR	& 4 OR LESS	LIMITED PITCHOUTS.	ZONE	NO PENALTIES.	BEST BACK
LESS	LIMITED	USE SIMPLE BASIC PLANS.		NO MISTAKES	
NO HAND OFF	HANDOFF	THAT HAVE SUCCEEDED.			
		QUICK KICK ON 3RD & LONG			
10	20	50	40	20	10

BEST PLAYS -- VS -- EXPECTED DEFENSES

DEFENSES		OPPONENTS
72	PASSES -- BOX 2, 8, 28, AND COMPANIONS	ROGERS SAND SPRINGS CENTRAL
	RUNNING -- 8 P.O., 24, 26, 28, 6 AND COMPANIONS	OKMULGEE
GAP	PASSES -- JUMP, 8 ROLLOUT	MOST TEAMS ON
8	RUNNING -- 24 OUTSIDE, 26, 26 P, 6 SP., 28 AND COMPANIONS	GOAL LINE.
71	PASSES -- JUMP, 28	MUSKOGEE
	RUNNING -- 22, 24, 26 AND OFFENCE IN GENERAL	
63	SAME AS 72 PLUS -- JUMP PASS AND PLAYS OVER CENTER	B-VILLE OKMULGEE
53 INSIDE	RUNNING -- 2Q, 22, 4X, 24 INSIDE, 28, 8P.O., COMPANION PLAYS AND RUNNING PASS	EDISON B-VILLE
SPLIT 6	Q.B. SNEAK, 2 Q AND 4X WITH FLANKER, AND OUTSIDE OFFENSE	

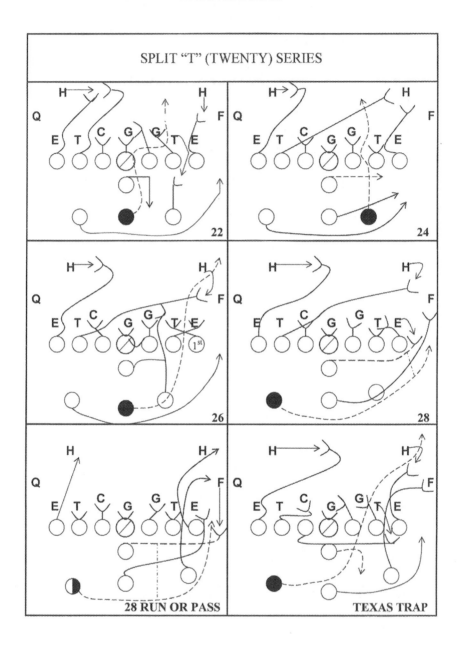

SPLIT "T" (TWENTY) SERIES

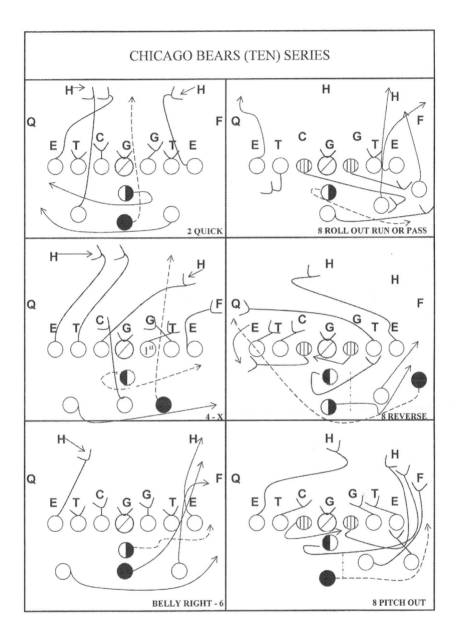

CHICAGO BEARS (TEN) SERIES

2 QUICK

8 ROLL OUT RUN OR PASS

4 - X

8 REVERSE

BELLY RIGHT - 6

8 PITCH OUT

SPECIAL PLAYS AND PASSES

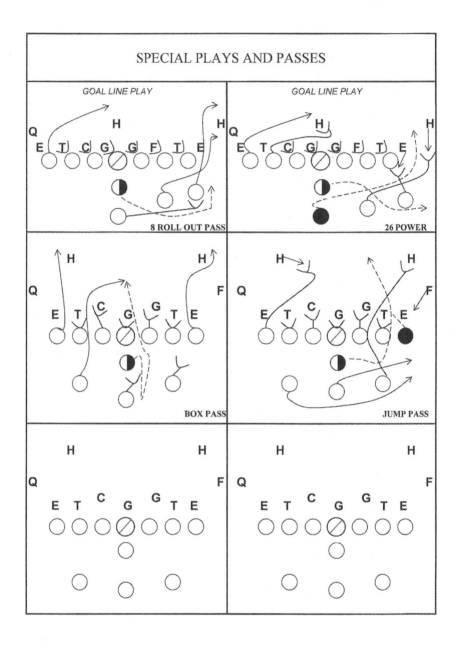

GOAL LINE PLAY

8 ROLL OUT PASS

GOAL LINE PLAY

26 POWER

BOX PASS

JUMP PASS

The Quarterback's Guide

In order for a quarterback to be outstanding, he must be cognizant of certain pertinent information relating to his offense, the opposition's defense, tactical and strategic information, and the principles of quarterbacking and field generalship.

Offensive, Defensive, and Tactical Information

The following information is the value and significance to the quarterback.

Information a quarterback must know about his own offense:

1. Know your teammates thoroughly, best pass receiver, best faker, best ball carrier, etc.
2. Know all of your plays and point of attack, blocking assignments.
3. Know where every receiver is on every pass pattern.
4. Know your best play and pass against every defense.
5. Know and understand how each play fits into a series.
6. Know and remember the plays that are working—keep running them.
7. Know the reasons for the proper line splits.
8. Know the plays the players have the most confidence in.
9. Know the best plays for special situations—draw, screen, etc.
10. Know how to stop the clock.

Information a quarterback must know about the defense:

1. What defense they are playing?
2. Who is making the tackles?
3. Are they stunting their defenses?
4. What type of pass coverage do they use?
5. Do the linebackers run through?
6. Are the ends crashing?

7. Who is tackling the passer?
8. Who is the best defensive man?
9. Which man can we best?
10. How quickly does the secondary revolve?

Information a quarterback must know about the game:

1. Time left to play is a big factor.
2. Timeouts left.
3. Weather and field condition.
4. Which down it is at all times.
5. How many downs to make? How many yards?
6. Field position.
7. What yard line the ball is on.
8. Which zone the ball is in—two-, three-, or four-down zone.

Wet field:

1. Play conservatively and kick early.
2. No difficult ball handling.
3. Avoid bad places on field, also wide plays and cut backs.
4. Do not be afraid to pass.

Free wheeling zone:

1. Try for long gainer.
2. Use sideline intelligently.
3. Use wind intelligently.
4. Use best ball carrier as decoy.
5. Utilize various formations.
6. Try long gainer on first down and go for first down on second down.
7. Call trick plays that have been set up earlier.
8. Try to keep ball in middle of field.

Quarterbacks must remember:

1. When you are ahead and the game is drawing to a close, play slowly, conservatively, and very deliberately.
2. When you are behind and the game is drawing to a close, play faster, be more reckless, and get the ball out of bounds to stop the clock.
3. When you are in scoring territory, you must score. Any yardage gained without scoring is of slight value only.
4. Any yardage you make deep in your own territory which does not serve to get the team into the free wheeling zone is of slight value.
5. If you are ahead by eleven points and there are not more than five minutes remaining to play and there is a strong wind against you, it is smart to take a safety instead of trying to punt our from inside your ten-yard line.
6. Time works with you when you are ahead and against you when your team is behind in score.
7. Figure what the defense would normally expect in any given situation, and then do the opposite.
8. If a play fails, you must know why.

Tips for quarterbacks:

1. You must have genuine confidence in yourself and your ability.
2. You must have the confidence and respect of your team.
3. You must have personality and leadership; then exercise it.
4. You must know the ability of your own personnel.
5. Play the percentages for ultimate team victory. Consequently you must study scouting reports and have a clear picture of the game plan. You must be able to recognize defenses immediately, and be able to direct your attack away from the strength of the defense. You should think with the defensive signal caller by putting yourself in his place. Remember it is a guessing game until you make a gain. After a gain you should be one play ahead of the defense.

6. Eliminate bad plays as they will defeat you. Only a fumble or a penalty can stop

your offense if you eliminate the bad plays.

7. Run more offensive plays by getting out of the huddle quickly.

8. After a penalty or a timeout, have your play called and the team ready to play at the line of scrimmage. Do not follow this procedure when trying to run out the clock.

9. Try to score in one play after a break-in effort to demoralize the defense. Should you follow this procedure several times and not be successful, discontinue it; otherwise, you will demoralize your own team.

When not to try for score:

1. Just before halftime, behind your own forty-yard line.
2. When you are running the clock out.
3. When you are preparing to give a safety.
4. When you have one down to make a first down–go for first down.

When to try to score in one play:

1. When you have mental edge on opponent following a blocked kick, a recovered fumble, or an intercepted pass in the opponent's territory.
2. Just before halftime in the opponent's territory.
3. On waste down in opponent's territory.

When to run your best ball carrier behind best blockers:

1. When you must have first down.
2. In four-down zone going in for a score.
3. Clutch down in danger zone, coming out.
4. Save your best ball carrier in the free-wheeling zone.
5. Do not use him first play after a long run.

What to do on clutch down:

1. Fake and give.
2. Some kind of an optional play.
3. Best ball carrier behind best blocker.
4. When trying to save time, tell ball carrier to go out of bounds.

Scoring area:

1. Best ball carrier behind strongest blockers.
2. First down inside three–run ball yourself. No ball handling.
3. Make sure that on fourth down you will have the ball in the middle of the field where you can try any type or a scoring play, or extra point.

What to run on waste down:

1. Safe, long gainers.
2. Fake-give or optionals are normally effective.

When to speed up offenses:

1. When you are behind.
2. Inside the opponent's fifteen-yard line.
3. When you have the wind to your back.

When to slow down your offense:

1. When you are trying to kill time.
2. Just before the half in your own territory and you are ahead.
3. Fourth quarter, if more than one touchdown ahead.
4. When the wind is against you.

The quarterback must do the following:

1. Understand and recognize defenses.
2. Relate our offense to each defense.
   a. Avoid the bad play – (go quickly)
   b. Run inside – outside – reverse or pass.
   c. Run a balanced offense. Example
      <u>Inside – Handoff -7 –Sneak – 3</u>
      <u>Outside – 7 times</u>
      <u>Reverse – 3 times</u>
      <u>Passes – 3 times</u>
3. Understand tactics
   a. Score – time remaining.
   b. How many downs and how many yards.
   c. Think what the defense will do then do the opposite unless you can do the logical well,
      1) If we have one down to make 8 yards they will expect a pass. We will hit the hand off. (They will be loose).
      2) Two downs to make 2 yards they will expect a T. D. play. We will pick up 1st down with sneak or hand off.
      3) Sometimes on 3rd and short in the 4 down zone we will run outside because they will expect an inside play.
      4) Avoid the bad play and when we must make yards we will run 1 and 2 Q, 23, 24 sneak or keep.
4. Be familiar with opponents
   a. Take advantage of defensive tactics.
      1) Run around crashing ends.
      2) Run inside deep penetrating tackles.
      3) Run around a tight line: Run through a loose line.
      4) Use reverse against a sliding or angle-charging line.
      5) Use cross blocking when possible, against a hard, straight charging line.
   b. Know who stopped your play.
      1) Use your own eyes.
      2) Get information from teammates.

      c.   Run a play at an injured opponent or a substitute: Throw a pass into the territory of an opponent who has just fumbled.

5.   Don't waste your time outs – use your opponents.

6.   Position on field.

      a.   From your own goal to the twenty yard line is the <u>danger zone</u>. From the opponents twenty yard line to their goal is the scoring zone. The remaining area is the neutral zone.

      b.   When in your danger zone do the following:

         1)   Get the ball out quickly and as safely as possible.

         2)   Inside your own ten yard line use QB sneak or keep and quickies with the fullback deep. Punt on third down.

         3)   Inside your own five yard line punt on second down if you have not made five yards.

      c.   When in the scoring zone do the following:

         1)   Use your most trusted play and the best ball carrier.

         2)   When inside the opponent's ten yard line our line must close the splits. You must never fail to score inside their ten.

         3)   On 3rd down and long yardage think about moving the ball to mid field for a 4th down field goal.

7.   On 27 and 28 stay on the outside hip of the fullback until he makes his block.

8.   On the running pass your route is between the Q.B. and fullback and toward the line of scrimmage. Always run when you can make four yards.

Chapter 4

Theory of Defensive Play

Our defensive team will be thought of as two units.

1. The forcing unit – usually a seven-man front. This unit must force the play and pursue the ball. *Gamble.*
2. The containing unit – usually a four-man deep situation. This unit must act like a large wheel by rotating and expanding when necessary.

The secondary should do the following:

Four Deep situation (72 def.)
1. Keep outside and deeper than all offensive players.
2. Keep the same relative position with the ball.
3. Never cover the flat until the ball is in the air. Allow a six-yard passing gain—prevent the long gain.
4. Rotate with flankers and to the wide side of the field in the following manner: (example on page 36.)

    On drop-back pass, all four deep men expand the diameter of the wheel by dropping back and out.

    Corner Linebacker – Never rotate closer than eight yards toward the sideline or past the hash mark going the other direction.

Halfback – Never rotate past the center of the field. The containing unit should be inconsistent on rotation. Do not always do the same thing. Occasionally wait until the ball moves—and then rotate.

Responsibilities for four-deep protection against running:

Corner linebacker – Turn the play in.

Fullback and center – Move with the quarterback. Stop anything inside your tackles. Force the running passer.

Halfbacks – Tackle inside the corner man on wide plays. Move with the wheel on all others. Find the ball.

Pass Defense (72 and 53)

The defensive center and fullback play close to the line of scrimmage; and as the pass play develops they move backward facing to their inside, the center being conscious of the left end and the defensive fullback being conscious of the offensive right end. Both of these secondary men should be on the alert for short passes to the ends in their territories. After the center is positive that the left offensive end is not to receive a pass in his territory, he turns his attention to the right offensive end that may come across into his territory. Fullback does the opposite.

The safety man should be a centerfielder on the football team. He should not play any one would-be receiver but should back up and play the ball wherever it is thrown and prevent the touchdown on runs. Rotate to the halfback on flankers and movement of the offensive backs.

The halfback is responsible for any receiver deep behind him to his outside. If a man enters the flat zone in front of the halfback, this defender should be given the responsibility of protecting against this man only after the pass has been thrown. He should keep his eyes on the passer at all times and keep ahead of any would-be receiver entering his zone.

72 Defense for Passing

C and F	Cover hook zone and flat when possible (running pass to opposite side).
CB	Cover as deep as possible and outside. Rotate to HB on offside pass.
HB	Let no man deeper than yourself. Cover the outside man when in doubt. (For example, when two receivers are entering your zone.) Rotate to mid-field when the opponents' backs flow away from you. (For example, running pass opposite side.)
Notice	In general, halfback responsibility is cover deep and outside unless the cornerback has the deep outside. When this happens you cover deep inside.
Ends	Hit the offensive end. Rush the passer from the outside on drop- back passes. Make the running passer throw the ball. You are the reverse man. You must keep the passer in the pocket.
Tackles	Rush the passer madly.
Mid-Guard	Prevent the draw play/screen pass and rush the passer.

53 Normal	Same as 72 except for the following:
LG	Play safety and cover deep middle.
HB	Play outside. Cover deep and outside.
CB	Cover shallow outside.
Center	Move with the offensive fullback or cover shallow middle.

Punt Coverage

When we kick, our punter will always be instructed to kick the ball for the sideline in an effort to place it out of bounds. However, there will be times when our kickers will not hit the sidelines, and we must avoid letting the opponents make long punt returns. We will cover kicks as follows:

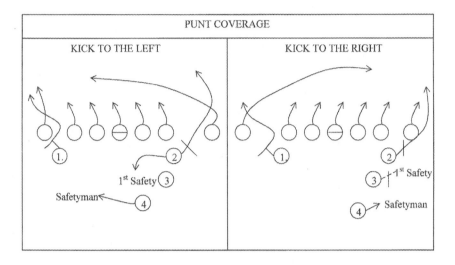

RE Go down field, and if the ball is kicked toward your sideline, drive for the ball carrier forcing him up against the sideline, and make every effort to tackle the ball carrier. Do not worry about turning the ball carrier in this situation. Rather, you should force him against the sideline and tackle him or drive him out of bounds. If the ball is kicked to the opposite sideline, you should protect your outside and drive the ball carrier against the far sideline. Again you should make very effort to tackle the ball carrier. If the ball is kicked down the middle of the field (this should not happen if we are getting good kicking) force the play and make an effort to tackle the ball carrier by forcing him to your inside.

LE Block if necessary but get down field a quickly as possible. Your instructions are exactly similar to those for the RE except you will be driving him into the left sideline if the ball is kicked to the left side or to the right sideline if the ball is kicked to the right side of the field.

C, G's, and T's Protect your area until you hear the ball hit the kicker's foot. Move down field fast, fanning out to cover the field adequately. With all of your speed, move in and make the tackle.

Backs 1 and 2 As soon as you have blocked, start down the field as quickly as possible. If the ball comes your way, *you must get to the outside and turn the ball carrier back into the field. It is your responsibility to never let the ball carrier get outside of you and be in a position to move down the sideline.*

Back 3 As soon as you have blocked, move down the field about three-quarter speed becoming the first safety man. You should not force the play but should be ready to move in on the tackle if the ball carrier breaks by our first line of defense.

Defense 70

1. All linemen move with the snap of the ball and make a *great second effort* if blocked.
2. Backs determine pass or run quickly by watching *their* ends. Then play the ball well.
3. *All men tackle hard enough to force fumbles.*

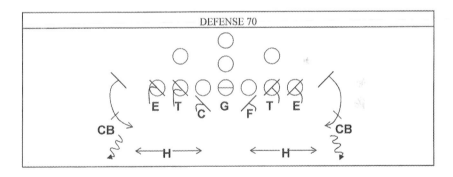

Ends Line up shading the outside of the offensive end. Charge hard straight into the end and drive him back being sure he does not block you in. Go to the ball. You are responsible for *leverage on reverse plays and drop-back passes.*

Tackles Line up shading the outside of the offensive tackle. Charge hard straight into the tackle and never let him block you in. Play the ball. Tackle any diving back.

RG Line up head on to the offensive center about one and a half feet off the line of scrimmage. Hit and control the center being sure that he does not cut you either way. Vary your methods and play soft now and then.

C and G Line up shading the outside of the offensive guard one yard off the line of scrimmage. React to the guard. Tackle any diving back. Note: You may "X" with your tackle when this signal is given. Be sure you deepen enough to shoot the gap properly.

Cornerback Line up four yards outside the offensive end and four yards behind the line of scrimmage.

1. If the end blocks, come across quickly and force the play being sure you turn the ball carrier in.
2. If the end does not block and HB moves away from you, *drop back deep and fast* keeping outside position on every man.
3. If the QB drips straight back to pass, drop straight back to cover the deep outside.
4. Key on side end and off side HB.

HB Line up on the inside shoulder of the offensive ends eight to nine yards back. Move with the QB keeping your same relationship wit him until you have determined pass or run. Then react fast to the play. Key ends for run or pass.

Goal Line Defense 80

(All linemen will take a four point stance.)

Ends Line up shading the outside of the offensive end and charge through him toward the fullback. Find the ball.

Tackles Line up in the *end-tackle* gaps and charge through the hip of the tackle. Find the ball.

Guards Line up in the *guard-tackle* gaps. Shoot the gap and find the ball.

FB and C Line up in *guard-center* gaps. Strike a blow, back out, and pursue or cover tackle to tackle passes.

LH and Q Line up four yards outside and deep from your end. Play like a cornerback on 72 defense. Exchange assignments with the end occasionally.

RH Line up six yards deep in front of the ball. Watch for a jump pass. Make the tackle.

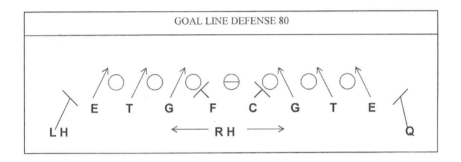

Adjustments to Offside Flankers for 72 and 83 Defenses

Ends

HB's   For an offside flanker do the following:

Cornerbacks

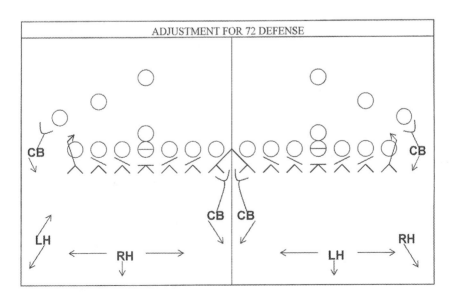

GOAL LINE DEFENSE 80

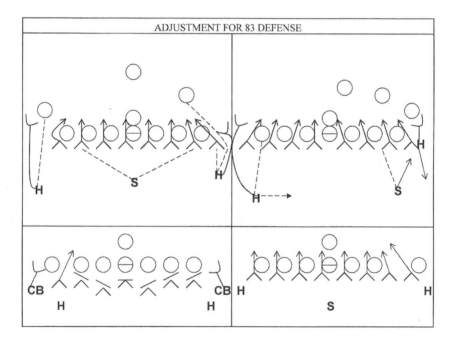

E   T   G   F   C   G   T   E

L'H   ←——— RH ———→   Q

1. For onside HB or FB flankers, our C. B. will move out and cover man for man.
2. For split ends our ends will move in and shoot the gap.
3. Defensive fullback and center give notice on flankers.

ADJUSTMENT FOR 83 DEFENSE

Spread Defense

We will use our victory (53) defense as a starting point for our spread defense.

MG Line up in front of the middle lineman.

Tackles Skip one man form the MG and play outside shoulder. Never split more than three yards.

Ends Line up on the next lineman's cut side shoulder or three yards. From your tackle if ends are split to the side line.

HB's Line up in front of the widest eligible receiver and nine yards deep.

CB's Line up in front of the second eligible receiver on your side and be four yards deep.

C Line up in front of the second eligible receiver on your side and be four yards deep.

Safety Play between your two halfbacks and twelve yards deep.

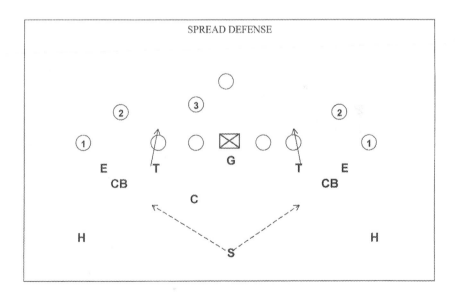

Chapter 5

Drills, Maneuvers, and Teaching Situations

Agility Drills

Quarter eagle, wave drills one and two, somersault and striking position, somersault and strike

Defensive Drills	Offensive Drills
Stance	Stance
Forearm and shoulder life	Blocking techniques
Forearm shiver	Extending
Forearm block	Board drills
Fighting pressure	Sled
Rolling out	Six-inch step
Leapfrog	Cross Charge
Submarining	Face the music
Cross face	Handclap drill
Coordination	
Angle of pursuit	

Offensive and Defensive Drills

One on one	Five on three
Two on one	Seven on five
Three on one	Circle drill

The five-on-three teaches blocking, forearm life, shiver, and personnel selection. The seven-on-five teaches assignments, the double team, trapping and avoidance of the last two, and pursuit angle.

Defensive situations

Tackle and mid-guard drill (three on five)
End drill (four on four)

1. Keep passer in pocket
2. Go to ball
3. Block for interception
4. Go to screen area
5. Prevent reverse

Wheel and shuffle drill, interception drill

Offensive situations

Counter, quickie, slant, option, reverse, running
Pass and drop back drills
When polishing offense or using drills:

    a. Place dummies off the scrimmage line.
    b. Place dummies where the opponents will be.
    c. Use live targets for option drills (ends and CB on 28).
    d. Men should hold dummies tough.

Many times the ball can be moved to avoid moving the dummies.

Methods of scoring on defense.

    a. Interception of a pass or fumble.
    b. Blocking and running with a blocked punt.
    c. Stealing the ball.
    d. Returning a punt or kick off.

Interception drill

Chapter 6

Scouting Rules

Follow the progress of each opponent during the weeks previous to scouting. Arrive on the scene early enough to hear local gossip and check evening paper.

Obtain a stadium seat high enough to see the whole picture. Be early enough to see the pre-game warm-ups.

If scouting with someone, have him write while you watch the offense, and while he watches the defense, you write.

We want the following information:

1. How did they win?
    a. Chart the plays they ran and how many times. Formations, pass patterns, and outstanding plays.
    b. Use the flankers, men in motion or passing?
    c. Are they stronger running or passing?
    d. Goal line play–most trusted back?
    e. Snap signal?
2. How can we stop their offense?
    a. Their opponent's most successful defense?
    b. Their offensive weaknesses and strengths?
3. How can we score?
    a. Who are their strongest backs? Linemen?
    b. Who are their weakest personnel?

4. Anything else that you deem necessary.
    Expenses will be paid by the school in the following:
    Car: going rate per mile and requisition money in advance or keep receipts.
    Meals: administration/athletic director determines amount per scout.

Glossary

Interior linemen—guards, tackles, center.

Exterior linemen—ends.

On side—point of attack

Off side—side away from attack; also in no-man's land before snap.

Strong side—side that has most men or right side on balanced formation.

Weak side—side that has the least men or left side on balanced formation.

No-man's land—length of ball.

First and ten—first down and ten yards to go (four downs to make ten yards.)

Leverage—keeping outside angle.

React—your movements depend on opponents' movements.

Pinch—slant in.

"X" blocking assignment—cross block, outside man first.

"Y" blocking assignment—block straight away.

"Z" blocking assignment—end and tackle block first man to the inside, guard pulls and blocks first man to show.

Defensive captain—defensive signal caller.

Peel—move to the play and block back

Screen block—prevent defensive man from pursuing.

Check block—block hard for one count then downfield.

Post block—check initial charge.

Power block—move man away from play.

Wedge block—interior linemen blocking straight ahead and to the inside.

Offense—we have the ball.

Defense—opponent has the ball.

"Red dog"—seven men rush.

Pass protection block—invite your opponent into a hole and hump him several times or rooster-fight him.

Kick protection—Turn to the inside and stand tough by resting your head on the inside man's hip. The center stands tough and square to furnish support for both guards. All backs protect the hole inside. (Diagram on page 13.) The center must practice passing the ball to the quarterback and punter each day until this can be done without error.

Theory Class
Of Tulsa Webster High School
Spring of 1955
Sixth hour after baseball season
Marv Martin, Jack Howard, Coaches!

Sam Terry, Coach Martin, Ron Lancaster, John Estes
Jerry Admire, Gary Smith, Bob Lancaster

Oil Bowl Cover

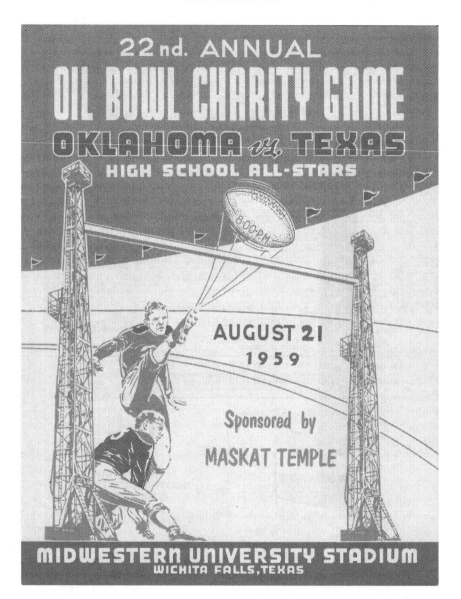

Scouting Charts

SCOUTING CHART

TEAM SCOUTED:	OPPONENT:	DATE:

TALLIES OF FLANKERS AND PASSES

| OFFSIDE LEFT | ONSIDE LEFT | | | OFFSIDE RIGHT | ONSIDE RIGHT |

LE	RE
LH	RH
FB	PSR

PERSONNEL

STRONGEST: WEAKEST:

1. _____   1. _____
2. _____   2. _____
3. _____   3. _____
4. _____   4. _____
5. _____   5. _____
6. _____   6. _____

REMARKS:

SCOUTING FORM

Attendance Chart

Student		M	T	W	T	F	M	T	W	T	F	M	T	W	T	F
	DAY															

Scouting Notes Page

The Religious Philosophy of Lewis "Cat Fish" Hayes

Lewis Hayes was my lifelong friend. The following was found in Lewis' wallet upon his death and given to me by his daughter.
Marv Martin

I would like to pass on to you the advice a chaplain gave his son upon graduation:

"I am giving you the ball son, and naming you the quarterback
For team in the game of life. I am your coach so I
Will give it to you straight. There is only one schedule to
Play. It lasts all your life but consists of only one game.
It is a long game with no time out and no substitutions.
You play the whole game all your life. You have a great
Backfield. You're calling the signals but the other three
Fellows in the backfield with you have great reputations.
They are called faith, hope, and charity.

You'll work behind a truly powerful line end to end. It
Consists of honesty, loyalty, devotion to duty, self
Respect, study, cleanliness, and good behavior.

The goal posts are the pearly gates of heaven, God is
The referee and sole official. He makes all the rules
And there is no appeal from them.

Author unknown – Scottish Rite News

About the Author

The author entered Northeastern State Teachers' College in the fall of 1946 after serving in the US Navy for three years. He was awarded a full athletic scholarship and started nine games as a freshman. His positions were right guard on offense and linebacker on defense. Also, his senior year he served as captain and called defensive signals, graduating in January 1950.

Beginning the 1951 football season, N.E. State selected Ken Due from West Point as the new head football coach. As a graduate assistant, the author served as assistant coach during spring practice.

In the summer of 1951, the author entered the University of Tulsa where he completed his master's in educational administration.

As a result of the N.E.S. college experience and the recommendation of Ken Due, in the fall of 1951 he was employed by Hal Wilson, the superintendent of Collinsville Schools in Collinsville, Oklahoma.

After spending two years at Collinsville, the author was employed by Tulsa Daniel Webster High School (at the time a 6A school) and the toughest conference in Oklahoma High School football during the 1950s and 1960s. After serving as assistant coach for four years, he was elevated to head coach in 1955. Taking over a program that lost more games than it won each year, the author rebuilt the football program and won six, lost four in 1958. The final game of the season was against the undefeated Edison High School team. As a result of the author's rebuilding of the football team of Webster High School, the Oklahoma High School Coaches Association selected him to coach the Oklahoma All Stars in 1958. (See the Oil Bowl Program in the index of the book.)

Note: Ron Lancaster played on the Webster football team and has written the preface for this book. Lancaster has served as a state championship coach in California and Oklahoma and his credentials are well-known by all.

Coach Martin went on to coach in high schools in Moore, Oklahoma, and Walnut Creek, California, where he had an undefeated season, and Folsom, California. It was in Folsom that he moved entirely into administration, beginning with his first principal's position at W.E. Mitchell Junior High. Mitchell Junior High was selected as one of the outstanding junior highs of the 1960s. He also administered schools in Stamford, Texas, and in Glencoe and Checotah, Oklahoma.

In 1971 Coach Martin became Dr. Martin after earning his doctorate in administrative education from the University of Arkansas in Fayetteville. He then began a career with the University of Arkansas Health Sciences as assistant to the chancellor.

Dr. Martin's lifetime passion for football is based on his belief that the sport has the potential for guiding young men throughout their life by teaching them the importance of teamwork, self-discipline, integrity, and hard work.